Interchange
and
Other Poems

Other works published by the author available from iUniverse:

Confusion Matrix and Other Poems (2007)
Surface Tension and Other Poems (2008)
War-Wise and Other Poems (2009)
Celebrations and Other Poems (2009)
Persistence and Other Poems (2010)
Pursuit and Other Poems (2011)
Black Hole and Other Poems (2012)
An Artist's Model and Other Poems (2012)
A Bell Curve and Other Poems (2013)
An Apology and Other Poems (2016)
The Longest Month and Other Poems (2016)
Summer in September and Other Poems (2016)

Interchange
and
Other Poems

DAVID J. MURRAY

INTERCHANGE AND OTHER POEMS

iUniverse books may be ordered through booksellers or by contacting:

iUniverse
1663 Liberty Drive
Bloomington, IN 47403
www.iuniverse.com
1-800-Authors (1-800-288-4677)

ISBN: 978-1-5320-8048-7 (sc)
ISBN: 978-1-5320-8049-4 (hc)
ISBN: 978-1-5320-8050-0 (e)

Print information available on the last page.

iUniverse rev. date: 10/09/2019

Contents

Wooing

Health and Age

States of Mind

A Vision in Black

Introduction

On my 78th birthday three years ago, I wrote the introduction to the first volume of a series presenting poetry written to a recently widowed friend. I had known her and her husband since the early 1970s, when he had been a professional colleague at Queen's University, Kingston, Ontario, Canada. They soon moved, however, to a university in the French-speaking province of Quebec. My wife, Esther, and I kept up a correspondence with them until February 2009, when Esther passed away.

Shortly afterward, I moved some 150 miles east from Kingston to Toronto to be closer to my grandchildren. Here I have an apartment with a patio overlooking the Scarborough Bluffs, a cliffside scenic conservation area of Lake Ontario at the eastern edge of Toronto. I had deliberately chosen to pass my retirement there in part because of the never-ending panorama of cloudscapes as the seasons progressed.

In the mid-1970s, my friend and her husband had bought a derelict farmhouse in Central Quebec. The house had no plumbing or electricity. Over the years, they renovated the house. It is surrounded by agricultural land and forest, as will be made clear in the poems.

My first volume in the series, *The Longest Month and Other Poems* (2016), was followed by *Summer in September and Other Poems* (2016). The poems in the latter volume describe some of the local travels my friend and I undertook between June and September 2015. The volume includes some poems about her place in Quebec and my place in Toronto. Later, to my delight, my friend occasionally wrote a poem of her own in reply to one of mine. These "pairs" of poems were assembled together in one of the sections that makes up *Summer in September*, namely, the section titled "Phone Calls and Letters." Our liking for these pairs of poems motivated us to consider writing a third volume in the series, which became the present work, *Interchange and Other Poems*.

As in *Summer in September*, *Interchange and Other Poems* is divided into ten titled sections, but *Interchange and Other Poems* contains a much larger proportion of stand-alone poems written by my friend. To be precise,

Interchange and Other Poems contains 55 poems written by her and 66 written by me. Among these, there are only six pairs of poems. As in *Summer in September,* all poems written by her are preceded by "She" in the text.

The first section, **Beginning,** contains one poem by each of us about how thought-provoking an experience it is to have a correspondence couched in verse as well as in prose.

Phone Calls contains ten poems by her and ten by me. The first poem is my reply to her poem about interchanges in Section 1. The remaining poems refer occasionally to her rural telephone service. My phone calls sounded to her like the crinkling of cellophane. This defect was caused by the humidity, which affected the functioning of her telephone line. When the cellophane is bad, we can't hear each other, so she has to try phoning again to find a clear line.

Grandchildren concerns my two grandchildren living here in Toronto with their mother (my daughter) and her husband. My friend wrote poems about the boy (then aged 8) and the girl (then aged 6). I wrote a poem describing my feelings when the train from Montreal to Toronto stopped at Kingston. From the right side of the train, I could see the trees of the cemetery where Esther's ashes are buried. My other poem, the first in the section, concerns a Hallowe'en festival held in the Guild Inn Park close to where I live. Both grandchildren participated in this event.

Winter has three poems by her and six by me. Her poem titled "Winter's End" needs explanation. Years ago a species of Asiatic ladybug (or "ladybird" in British English) was imported for agricultural pest control. These insects have more than two black dots on each of their red wing-cases and are more aggressive than the engaging little two-dot ladybugs we both grew up with. At the end of winter and at the end of summer, they can often be found indoors, where they congregate in large clusters. Two more poems by my friend about this ladybug plague are found in the section on **My Kitchen** below.

Animals has seven poems by her and eight by me. It is mainly about her pets. At the time these poems were written, she had three cats and one dog. The dog, a Labrador retriever, died in the spring of 2017 and has been replaced by a hybrid poodle puppy who is the star of her poem "Puppy Graffiti." There was also a stray tomcat which slept in a neighbour's stable and included my friend's house in his territory. He caused consternation among her pets by staring through the windows. My friend named him Chuckee

Cheese; he has now vanished. Two of the primary causes of accidental death among domestic pets in her neighbourhood are speeding cars on country roads and predation by coyotes. Another poem, "Queen of Bitches," describes a mongrel named Teesh, whom my friends owned decades ago.

Your Kitchen has seven poems by her and three by me. Her poems include the two about ladybugs already mentioned. One poem refers to Bill Bryson's book about walking the Appalachian Trail, and another poem concerns a meat grinder my friend couldn't disassemble so that it would fit into its drawer. I mainly rhapsodize about her cooking.

Wooing has eleven poems by her and eight by me. There are three pairs of poems in this section. Her poem "Many Thanks" alludes to the fact that I frequently shopped in Toronto for English-language books and classical music recordings that were difficult for her to find locally.

Health and Age has seven poems by her and nine by me. There is one pair of poems in this section. The cellophane problem in landline phone reception resurfaces.

States of Mind has six poems by her and nine by me. Her poem "Letter to the Bard" struck me as strange when I first read it, but she explained to me that the first fifty or so of Shakespeare's sonnets refer to his belief that once a woman ages and loses her looks, she is pretty much worthless. This advice, given by Shakespeare to his young male patron, sounded to my friend repellently misogynistic.

A Vision in Black was inspired by an incident in a Toronto tapas bar. My friend was wearing a black tunic and black slacks, which showed off wonderfully a gold-coloured necklace she had bought at a flea market on a trip we had made to Washington, D.C., in April 2016. In the bar, after a while, she wanted to stand rather than sit. I misinterpreted her move as an opportunity to model herself, because she seemed to be "posing" for me as she stood up. Nothing could have been farther from the truth. She has a back problem that makes it physically painful to sit for long periods, and she therefore has a need to stand up occasionally. On the basis of this somewhat pathetic situation, I wrote a theme and eight variations.

The last variation concerns another memory from our Washington trip. In a museum, we had seen in a glass case an open drawer revealing many tiny treasures, including a small book whose centre pages had been hollowed out; a small key lay in the resulting space. I think it is fitting that my friend rounded off **A Vision in Black**, and thereby the whole volume, by a short but telling poem about that book.

Acknowledgments

As in previous volumes, I am indebted to the people at iUniverse, and to Marty Cain and Wynona Owens in particular, for their cooperation and skill in preparing *Interchange and Other Poems* for publication. I also thank Rachel Breau for her help in the final stages of production. But particular thanks are owed to my friend for *her* contributions. She has insisted that *Interchange and Other Poems*, like all my previous volumes, bear my name as sole author. I would prefer it otherwise.

Beginning

Interchange

Brains 'n' blood 'n' skulls 'n' stuff
Can easily transported be
Through field and forest, farms and streams,
And even o'er the stretching sea.

How is stressed by math and science,
Why by the humanities.
When *interchange* I choose to use,
I'm talking of vocalities.

I mean the depth of wondrous words
Spoken as a symphony,
Of your telephoned voice alerting me
To all the great cacophony

That nature lavishes on her lands:
The wingbeats of the honeybee,
Coyotes' yelps and songbirds' calls,
The sounds of crass normality.

Interchanges

She:

You have shaved shreds
From your surface,
Hauled up embers
From your past,
Dived your oyster beds
For pearls of purpose,
And generously cast them
Forward for me to take
And strew their mayhem
Straight into my hissing wake.

How long will it be
Till those pearls
Before swine
Evolve from debris?
New thoughts unfurl
And recombine,
Travelling down
The telephone line
That links your lofty court
To far-off earthy mine.

Afterward, I lob them
Back toward you,
And with patient sigh,
You tweak them.
Now that they are fresh and new,
You swat them back at me,

Wondering, perhaps, if
I'll haw and hem,
Even detect a whiff
Of distant familiarity.

Phone Calls

Reply to "Interchanges"

When signs of death spread quickly
But, quicker, die away,
The better seems the sunrise,
Sign of a routine day,
When all the normal things I try to do
Seem tedious and trite, except when I'm
Electrified because I'm hearing you.

But if night's fiery chariot
Could lift me from my day
With all its mundane blah,
And sweep me far away
From all the duties that I can't get through
And to an Eden where I'd hear you all the time,
I'd know that night could make my dream come true.

I Hope That Time ...

I hope that Time will never clip my wings!
Life without your flammatory voice
Would be as empty as a grave-dug hole
And useless as a framework for my soul.

You speak, and airwaves spin and agitate
To send your original treasures to my ear;
Life without your sultriness of voice
Would leave me having very little choice

Of other sounds to listen to that turn
The spigots of my ageing spirits on
The way your breathy vocalizings do.
I love the conversations shared with you.

And when you speak, something inside me sings
That Time will find it hard to clip my wings.

Consolation

She:

The wind has stripped my ash of leaves
But left the twiglets bearing seeds
For possible multiple progeny.

The bus has whisked away my guest
And born him homeward to the west;
The curve of the earth hides him from me.

My ash will know another spring.
The bus to me my guest will bring
For probable multiple poetry.

But from the em'rald west may fly
A boring pest which may well try
To thwart Nature's plan for my ash tree.

As each ash leaf will feed the soil,
My eye shall fall upon the coil
Of the cord to telephone-calls-to-be.

And thus, at last I am consoled
(For both of us have grown quite old)
By the promise of future complicity.

Evening Phone Call

I always sit entranced by what you say.
Whether you speak to me softly or loudly, or whether you laugh,
Your voice is like a sonic autograph,
A signature closing the confines of my day.

During an Evening Phone Call

Pour me your sweetest wordings in mine ears
That we confound the deepest of our fears,
And let the ancient rules of war and wooing
Ward off whatever threatens our undoing.

Omitting an Evening Phone Call

A wizened worry-wart I'd be
If I took too much to heart my omission
To ask you earlier for your permission
To phone you at ten, when you'd hear from me
A heartfelt "good night" and a wish you'd sleep free,
Yet I still feel a need to express my contrition.

Your Horoscope

Within your horoscope lie simple signs
Augmenting what the prosodies of seers
Have cumulated in their books: designs
Prophetic that go back for years and years.

But you have signs unique to you that call
Your name a subtle candidate for psalms.
Readings are taken of the lines that sprawl
Across the heavenly heartlands of your palms.

Teacups are read and crystal globes divined,
And ancient Babylonian sagas sigh
Across the centuries to reach your mind
And spread your future over their desert sky.

But all I need to know of you I know
From hearing how our conversations flow.

Mounting Exasperation

She:

Though no equestrienne, I
Ride high on wooing's pony
And fear that by and by,
Though I can tell a phony
From the true hoofbeat
Of the ardent beating heart,
I shall be bucked off at your feet,
And you won't give a fart—
The swain once more the victim
Of the sorry nag that kicked him.

Like Jack and Jill, alas, alack,
I shall tumble down
And, worse than Jack,
Shall *lose* my crown
You so lovingly placed upon my hair.
And you'll retreat in Poet's funk,
Scribbling poems in your lofty lair
Of a suffering Wagnerian monk,
Of the slights and trials the world inflicts
And the nasty mare with nastier kicks.

So! Imagine my surprise:
Last night you told me
You firmly feared I'd heed
Another's roving eyes
Which might behold me
Astride my high and mighty steed.
Not *I* a-wooing will I go—

Nor other wooers will I prize—
For it's *your* wooing that rings my wealth,
And it's your *wooing* that rights your health.

So, listen up, Mr. Murray!
Don't you be in such a scurry
To cinch me to your heart's design.
I've *told* you I'd be your valentine.
The thought of other swains disgusts me.
Why on earth can't you trust me?
Do you think me flighty and fickle,
That with every phone call you must tickle
My tastes and flatter my ego,
Lest my fancies make me sea-go?
No! I'm quite happy on this farm
And truly proud to take your arm.

This evening's minutes I must count
Till you place me back upon my mount.

Reply to "Mounting Exasperation"

Some blackish clouds, like puffs of smoke,
Crawled on a backcloth made from gold
Set by the sun, till darkness rolled
Over my lake its evening cloak.

But that was after your letter arrived.
It was a poem. I truly believe
It's one of the finest I'll ever receive.
In a phone conversation I'd somehow contrived

To make you think I might be afraid
That someone would put my wooing to waste.
On reading my poem, I felt disgraced
That I such ignorance had displayed

And from my wooing been blown off course.
But I didn't fret! I shall rebound!
I'll write you sonnets that so resound
Through my lakeside cloudscape that I'll force

Angelic hordes to a battery
Of supersonic flattery.

The Softness of Your Voice

The softness of your voice sends tiny wakes
Of flitting water through my awakened mind;
No physics or geometries can find
Excuses for the hold your whispering takes
On the cauldron of my waking daytime brain.
I want to hear you over and again.

And when lush nighttime falls upon the snow,
Your voice may be quiet, but its afterimage stays,
Assuming many facets of the ways
Your voice follows your will, which knows to go
To a resonating chamber in my head
Where the softness of your voice is echoed.

So soft "good nights" I whisper cautiously
As night unfolds its velvet majesty.

Plastic Dinosaur

She:

Northern Telecom at our service here—
Creamy beige casing, clear plastic dial,
Solid servant to tongue and ear
When seasonal cellophane* does not defile
Or crop each word we utter, each one we hear.

I imagine you there, taking your seat
At a comfortable angle to your little table,
Where ear of listener and eye of beholder often meet.
Behind you, silent numbers scroll through cable
Down screen and never compete with our evening treat.

In these digital days, a dial telephone
Stymies the young but comforts the old,
For its clear acoustics (dare I own?)
Never break up and never withhold
The merest inflection of a loved one's tone.

My phone, at five years plus three score,
From the Salvation Army, has survived many falls.
Its digital replacements died hitting the floor.
The high-fidelity way to receive your phone calls
Is to hang onto my plastic rotary dinosaur.

---

* Wet weather to the west of where the poem's speaker lives causes a sound like cellophane crackling on the line.

Mixed Blessing

She:

I missed the news tonight; oh boy!
All doom and gloom without the joy.
And tho' my day seems incomplete,
I must admit it feels a treat
To skip the edited evening news
With limited angles and points of view.
So why on earth the sense of guilt
In not measuring the blood that's spilt?
I'm surely better away from it all,
Waiting for your telephone call.

Disconnected

Your house is by no means a citadel,
But that's what I felt when my telephone fell
And I cut us both off and had to redial,
Which wouldn't have been any kind of a trial
If I'd not also knocked, right under my chair,
The card with your house plan I always keep there
Showing what's northeast or southern or west.
Until that moment I'd never have guessed
That when I retrieved the card somewhat later,
I'd suddenly feel like an arch-desecrator
Who, by dropping that card with its bearings prodigious,
Had behaved like an oaf who had been sacrilegious.

Time Apart, Time Together

She:

Hours and hours
We spend alone.
Ours and ours alone
Are the jars and jars
Of words we pour
Down the telephone,
Those hours and hours …
Never alone.

Posy Good Night

She:

The ditch iris
Flagged me down,
Entreating entry
To my cool kitchen's vase
On the dormant wood stove.
"Let us join
Your ox-eye daisies
With their open yellow eyes.
We will mix
With pansies blue,
With pansies white
And pansies cream and mauve."
So I yielded
To their plea, and
To my eyes' delight,
They will not wilt
Till I wish you good night.

Your Voice Is There Again

Your voice is there again. A hidden force
Embellishes its boldness as I hear
Narrations of your day's events. The rain,
The mud, the traffic, all delight my ear.

A subtle darkness permeates your voice.
Proclivities they portend where you advance
Things that are everyday and commonplace
To status heights that spur me to elevate

Whatever you say about twigs or tubs or trees
To sublimity and significance.
And even disparagements serve to raise
What's humdrum to a new magnificence.

And so I press my ear into the phone.
Your voice keeps all my inner hopes alive.
Its sounds go gallivanting through my brain
And guarantees my longings for you thrive.

Unbound Words

She:

Sometimes our fantasies
Of us together
Differ so widely
That I chuckle.
You, with carnal lustiness,
Might tether your dreams
To a bedpost.
As for me?
Strolling mildly
Through your *Chambers's*,*
I see you uncover
A host of my treasures
Loosely contained in *Webster's*.**
Our dictionaries buckle
Under the stress of use.
Their covers unfettered,
Fadingly lettered
And battered,
Pages adrift.
To rebind or not?
Impossible for me
To cut the knot,
To release Webster
From my keeping
To binder's ministrations
Without weeping.

---

* *Chambers's Twentieth Century Dictionary*, 1943 edition.
** The speaker of the poem keeps all her dictionaries in her kitchen.

Tachistoscopic Flash

She:

With a deft twist
Of a knife blade,
Handle firm in fist,
I opened a packet
Of Scottish shortbread.
In its homemade bracket
The light bulb overhead,
Needed for this task,
Caught the blade's flash,
Bounced it off the door glass
And flung it at my eye,
Which leapt to see
Who had just dashed by.
Nothing out there in the dark.
Just the door glass reflecting me.

Shortbread fingers
With a cup of tea …
Still the image lingers
Tachistoscopically.
My thoughts wander west.
I wonder if your hold
On Kant's metaphysics
Has insistently been wrested
From sturdy mind's grasp
By family* so bold
That theories and measures mix

_____

*   My friend wrote this on New Year's Eve when I was with my family in Toronto.

With cherished kinship's clasp.
Will you phone at seven-thirty,
Or will it be at half past nine?
Will you feel tired but flirty
When you tell me all or nothing is divine?

Ear of the Listener Meets Eye of the Beholder

She:

Lack of propinquity
Has sharpened my ear.
I hear what I don't see,
When each evening
The miles disappear,
Your presence receiving.

Easier for me than for you:
My interlocutor
Need not be in view,
Subject to my constant gaze.
You cannot pocket her,
Hidden from your eyes, ablaze

With stupendous avidity,
But must place her within your sight,
Watching the grace and fluidity
Of her every move and the drape
Of her garment—dull or bright.
From your urge to see, there seems no escape.

I often wonder if my failure
To express my admiration
Of the cock of your head, your natty regalia,
Or the slender elegance of your form
Meets with disappointed resignation.
No appreciative compliments swarm

Like pollen grains to your psyche.
If so, please remember that in *my* mind,
I gain entry to your realm, where my key
Unlocks the coffer with all its trappings,
Disclosing your treasure. After all, I'm not blind.
I can sense your mood in a throng, despite its wrappings.

Alluring Routine

She:

There's the rosary from radio heaven
Rumbling away in the cellar.
I find its rise and fall comforting,
As I know it's not yet seven.
Not time yet for that feller
In his tower on his lake
To phone and start cavorting
In my mind, for heaven's sake.
And yet my pulse quickens:
Quick! Quick! It tick-ticks.
Time to turn down the chickens,
Leash up the pup to do her tricks,
Turning the snow a lovely yellow
Before I converse with the gallant fellow.

Grandchildren

Hallowe'en at the Guild Inn Park

Hobgoblins, ghouls and ghastly ghosts
Flit and run around the park
While the brilliant orange-crested trees
Stand sentinel against the dark
Of a dark oncoming rain-filled cloud
That threatens to subdue the crowd.

Indeed, when it rained, a werewolf began
To move to a tent to be photographed.
A zombie princess painted her name,
Leaving her pumpkin autographed.
And a girl dressed up as Superman
Licked a lollipop as she ran.

But I thought how pleased *you'd* be to see
How so many tree trunks had blackened bark:
The rain had painted them ebony,
Which made them stand solid and stark
Against the light of a leafy fall
Where death could not be seen at all.

Grandson

She:

In silent concentration bent,
He builds with brittle plastic blocks,
Composing in his element,
Where every parcel interlocks.
Once a bird, today a ketch.
We admire it from every angle.
Tomorrow, will we see him stretch
To a Learian* Quangle Wangle?**

---

*   Refers to Edward Lear (1812–1888), English painter and nonsense poet.
** A nonsense creature occurring in Edward Lear's nonsense writings

Granddaughter

She:

When a dancer hears music,
All turf beckons to her feet.
All these are her bailiwick:
Carpet, parquet and concrete;
Mossy forests, firm-packed beach
And Mississippi mud—
All await her body's reach.
Dancing's in her blood.

Kingston Station, November 6, 2016

Their grandmother is there; she does not know I'm here.
Darkness shrouds the waiting woods of November
And does nothing at all to dictate what I remember.

No hiding place can couch my silent heart.
I think of her neither knowing I am near her
Nor knowing how her grandchildren revere her.

Winter

Forecast

A tiny scattering of snow
Reminds us all, down here below,
That high up there, high in the sky,
Winter demands that summer must die.

Where You Lie Asleep

I look at the misty hair that decorates
The resilient pillow where you lie asleep,
And I see a thousand filaments that keep
You warm when Old Man Winter infiltrates.

Likewise, a thousand airwaves make each word
That fills this hymn to ever-perennial you.
In every line of words each thought runs true,
And any discomposure sounds absurd.

Your Winning Ways

She:

A glance
At the calendar
Shows
One more row
Of pristine snows
To hoe.

But you,
Nobody's fool,
Need no tools
Nor cramponed boots
To school
Winter's jewels,

For now
You live high
Above
Us small fry
And dream of love …
Satisfied.

Was then
That winter sport
Always a chore?
Snow athwart
Your drive …
In drifts galore!

Perhaps
You aspired
To chickadee praise
As they admired
Your winning ways
With winter?

Entranced, I Watched You Move From Room to Room

As the cold days of winter pass away
And mornings dawn increasingly warm and clear,
I think of that interminable May*
Before you took the train to see me here.

Entranced, I watched you move from room to room.
Enlivened, I heard your footsteps in the hall.
Excited, I'd thought I'd have to stave off gloom
Recalled, but this was not the case at all.

Instead, each day was filled with new events,
Discoveries of things we liked together.
Each day brought out from me new compliments
No matter what the wind or sun or weather.

I still reflect, with pride and with relief,
That my feelings for you still beggar my belief.

---

*   Mentioned in "The Longest Month," David Murray, *The Longest Month and Other Poems*, Bloomington, IN: iUniverse, 2016, p. 2.

Letting Winter Go

She:

Do I yearn
To give up
Winter Wednesday meals
Of Atlantic salmon
And endless reels of backgammon
So as to grab
The Arctic char
From the fishmonger's slab?
At last I'll stow
My splitting axe
And address myself
To income tax.

Next Year's Snow

When next year's gently falling snow announces
The furnishing of lake-soft waves with flounces
And covers the land with mantles of pure white
Like moonlit-washed reflections in the night,
I'll treat that snow as a foretaste of delight.

Later, the beauty your every move displays
Will mirror the summer's retinue of days
And thereby leave, in my memories of you,
Addenda from activities we'll do.
Each concept heard, each arc of vista view,

Each slow relinquishment of coloured light
As the sun bowed down to introduce the night,
Each open space we'd dare to occupy,
Each cloud that lined the sweeping breadth of sky,
Will yield me pleasures you will multiply.

Winter's End

She:

Oh, Lord, I know
That spring
Is not far away
When a ladybug
Drops down
Off the ceiling
Into my mug
Of cafe au lait.

The Cold

The weather's up and down now, and the cold
Exposes herself quite unremittingly
Whenever the sun shines intermittently,
Proving to all her pride at being bold
And refusing to act according to what she's told.

But she can give her sadism some slack.
A hint of warmth rebounding from tall towers,
A glint of an Easter shop that's selling flowers,
A notice that the nights are keeping track
Of signs of spring, all state that April's back.

These render her less ready to defy.
She has no need for merciless exhalations
Loaded with envisioned devastations.
She can subside and content herself to sigh
Like Psyche watching Cupid wander by.

End of Winter

I see the weeping willows on the hill
Turn from a youthful yellow into jade
Before the other verdures re-parade
The onset of a new spring's accolade.

And every year that I shall see you still
Being your old traditional self, I'll know
You'll know renewal when warmer breezes blow
And when the fresh and burgeoning saplings grow
New branches to dapple new carpetings of snow.

I know that growing acquaintance will not shade
The primary pull that genuinely drew
Me to the true delight that you conveyed
When spring's wide world endeared itself to you.

Animals

You and Your Cats

You will I festoon with verses made
Of mellifluity adapted less for you
Than for your voice, which pulls this accolade
Of verbal reciprocities into view.

For after you've made your way toward your fridge,
Or tidied up the scraps that your cats had dropped,
I've heard your voice extol the privilege
Of watching over those "children" you had kept

(From frozen farm or regulated shelter)
To educate them in a den you'd made,
Where they enjoyed a life they'd never alter,
Given the affection you've displayed.

For you to leave would be, for them, abandonment,
Loss of the loveliest voice in any feline firmament.

Frozen Assets?

She:

With mounting frustration, I nearly wept,
While Fur-Fur watched and Willow slept
As Chuckee* left his frozen piss,
A signature that looked amiss
Upon my south-facing windowpane,
An unwelcome reminder, this horrid stain,
That Chuckee triumphs yet again.

---

* In Quebec most apartment dwellers' leases end on the first of July. If their new leases ban household pets, many tenants "chuck" their pets in the remote countryside before, or shortly after, this date. Chuckee Cheese, as the speaker of this poem called the cat, resisted capture for three winters before a speeding car put him out of his misery. Willow was her Labrador retriever. Fur-Fur Girl is her tortoiseshell cat who prefers variable spellings of her name.

Four Mother's Day Cards to You From Your Pets

From Mr. Pavarotti in the Spring

O cara mia! Mama! Aspetta qui!
All these are songs I sing whene'er I want to pee
And ask you to hold an open door for me
To sidle out and sing a melody
To the peepers and the froggies in your pond
And then *Addio!*, of which they're very fond.

From Furr-Furr in the Summer

This summer will prove to be a purr-purr whirl.
From Abby, my name has changed to Furr-Furr Girl.
My sister Tibby has a cunning name,
Based on Abitibi's wood pulp fame.
But Abby's a name distasteful to my ear;
Furr-Furr's the name I far prefer to hear.

From Tibby in the Fall

The leaves turn red, the brushwood's looking dead,
But I keep looking for the cat I dread,
One Chuckee Cheese, as he's called. And when I see
Him loitering at the window eyeing me,
I climb on the table where you're writing now
And shatter your attention with "miaow!"

From Willow in the Winter

Though tired, I feel my legs, when going uphill,
Stir to life when I know that I'll get back
To my comfy kitchen chair, from where I will,
With ageing sentinel eyes, keep careful track
Of when your movements tell me you will go
Out with me for a resniff of the snow.

Queen of Bitches

She:

Back in the days
When we measured in miles
And froze in Fahrenheit,
We lavished praise
On her canine wiles.
She was black and white.

We called her Teesh.
Canine freedom reigned
Way back then.
No need for a leash.
Dogs, sometimes restrained,
Yielding to randy yen,

Would chew lines and ropes
Or, if chained, drag their niches
Across irrigation ditches,
Up and down slopes,
To show up at Teesh's
And court the Queen of Bitches.

Our lucky Jacques Cartier terrier!*
The vet who spayed her
Missed a bit,
Leaving life merrier

---

* As far as I know, there is no such breed. My friend and her husband coined the term to refer to Quebec mongrels of centuries' standing.

For those who laid her,
A lineup to her credit!

Cold and weary, Teesh jumps up and begs
Entry. She and Paco cross the floor.**
Together they lie, quiet as mice,
While rejected swains lift their legs
Against our west storm door,
Sealing us in with yellow ice.

He made himself at home, that Paco,
A gracious gentlemanly type,
Stretched out beside the fire.
Ridding its dottle of tobacco,
He chewed quietly on Dad's pipe
Next to his object of desire.

In our barn built for pigs,
Teesh ran her estival inn—
Kibble in trough, water in pond.
They performed their coupling jigs
Until a car, out for a spin,
Dispatched her Paco to the great beyond.

And now global warming
Steams us in Celsius degrees,
While hectares measure our riches.
No more swains a-swarming—
Tall, short, eager to please,
To court the Queen of Bitches.

** Paco was Teesh's preferred suitor.

Homeward Bound

She:

My mind's eye spies
On your homeward-bound train.
It comes as no surprise
To see you rapt again
With wonder at the view
(And veggies hard to chew).

My own trip home,
After seeing you board the bus,
Beneath the wide blue dome
Entailed almost no fuss.

My heart skipped a beat
When I spotted, black and still
Against the curb's concrete,
Today's feline roadkill.

Beloved Boston Blackie
Has purred his last *ron-ron*;*
He met his Cadillacky
*Au pied de notre pont.***

---

*   French for "purr-purr."
**   French for "at the foot of our bridge."

Hurt Feelings

She:

For five whole nights
I was gone
To foreign sod,
Where, under city lights,
I stayed.*
This morning I trod
The spongy lawn
To transverse ditch
Where you had laid
Your froggy spawn—
Forty-three egg balls which
Crowned a week of delights.

Not one note
Of amorous chatter
Signalling your fecundity
Reached my distant ear,
Nor this morning
A single croak.
I wish it didn't matter
That I missed your mating song
This year
And that, this morning,
Not one of you spoke
Of your vernal ecstasy.

---

*   Addressed to the frogs, upon our return from Washington, D.C.

A Jungle Creature (Tibby)

A jungle creature catching petals
Is what your cat is when she catches
Deadheaded flowers with yellow patches,
Each afloat before it settles
Gently near the softness of her paws.

And you I see with your arms uplifting
When, from all your outstretched fingers,
Each yellow deadhead quietly lingers
Before it rises, then starts sifting
Downward toward the catch-net of her claws.

And so once more you're Aphrodite,*
But now you're in green and tossing flighty
Showerings of one-shot petals
To be caught by your cat before each settles.

---

* Mentioned in "You as Wedding Guest," David Murray, *Summer in September and Other Poems*, Bloomington, IN: iUniverse, 2016, p. 76.

But Then

Once, I wished that you'd travelled
Here on a magic carpet
From far away, where you were,
To be here, where I sat and listened.
I'd have held your imagined hand
And swung your imagined arm
And taken you out for fine dining.
But then
You'd be torn away from your animals.
Guilty, I'd suddenly stopped
And cut off such talk to myself.

No, you still reside out there,
And when you did phone me here,
Your voice was addictively soft
As you listed all the legumes
You had lavished on your supper
And spoke of sautéed eggplant
That you had had for lunch.
But then
Willow saw Chuckee, intruder,
And barked so loudly that you dropped
The phone. I was cut off again.

Puppy Graffiti

She:

A milky swoosh
Of canine noseprint,
Enthusiastic daub:
Pup's first graffiti
On the lower south pane.
Can I bring myself
Ever to wash
Her excitement
From the window
Onto her world?

Midnight Neglect

She:

Guilt dogs me.
So long
Since I've beheld
A fully spangled night sky,
Since my eyes' mind
Feasted upon
Greeting
Constellations
Instead of
Attending
To canine
Urinations.

A Swallowtail

Clouds broke the mighty breathing space of sky.
A swallowtail, adventuring, sailed by,
Hesitated, sun-specked, flitting and swooping,
In near-parabolas and arcs of looping,
And swift entrancing acts of daring, darting
With sudden downward drifts before departing
Up and away again in scan and weave,
Until it descended into a reprieve
From movement. Its wings, quiescent in their black,
Lay silently open, inert and flat and slack,
Waiting until it found itself secure
To mount and retest the wind's allure,
And, free to excel in coursing through the air,
Indulge in the joy of being there.

Happy Birthday From Mrs. Swindon Swallowtail

She:

Dearest Mr. Murray, Sir:
My Swindon swain*
Claimed your terrain
As nuptial rendezvous,
And our courtship
On your cruise ship
Finally did come true.
Oh, birthday boy,
'Twas not our joy
To wed in front of you.
But even so,
I still bestow
Greetings from us two.
Sincerely,
Mrs. Swindon Swallowtail.

---

* A tiger swallowtail butterfly claimed Mr. Murray's terrace as his territory. We called him "Swindon Swallowtail." We never saw his bride.

Your Kitchen

A Riddle: Who Am I?*

She:

In my realm I'm one of the world's hottest chicks,
Where ninety-nine is constant, as are seventy-seven and sixty-six;
Where one hundred eleven equals seventy-one.
And you should see what I have done
With a simple two-twenty-two …
Melt your heart? Or thaw your stew!

True, you can bring the world to its adoring knees
With all eighty-eight of your very own keys,°
But where in the world would you ever float
Without my single piercing note?
I admit that I'm not much of a cuddle,
But without me you'd be in such a muddle!

Who am I?

°   Answer: a microwave oven. What one keys in on the keypad does not always equal the number of seconds of heat produced. Murray plays the piano. It has eighty-eight keys.

A Paean to Your Food

For parsleyed eggs that never knew a flaw,
For duck breast cubes bestrewn with chanterelle,
For sturgeon fortified by cheese delight,
I write these lines of thanks the world to tell.

For steak so succulent it melts one's mind,
For pairings of ripe pears and mirabelles
Flared into beds of grapes-and-berries joy,
I write these lines of thanks the world to tell.

For cabbage sliced to slabs of brightest green
In melted butter laid by a citadel
Of pork and beans, exorbitant in appeal,
I write these lines of thanks the world to tell.

Your food is cooked so wonderfully well.
I idolize its flavour and its smell.

Mountain Range and Table Plain

She:

In Bryson's Appalachian walk,[*]
He writes about millennia of geology,
Multiple collisions continental
And a possibility of four ice ages.
On my kitchen table's plain
Lie paper layers at which I balk,
Accumulating for archaeology.
And for reasons mostly sentimental,
I resist shifting the strata of your pages.

---

[*] See Bill Bryson, A *Walk in the Woods*: *Rediscovering America on the Appalachian Trail*, New York: Broadway Books, 1998.

Invitation

She:

Can you imagine the Easter Bunny
With his basketful of eggs
On a March day, clear and sunny,
Sauntering along on muscular legs
That nature designed as wiry hoppers?
His eggs—Fabergé would weep—
Certainly *are* splendid showstoppers!
Studded with chocolate dark and deep,
Crystallized ginger a-wink in the sun,
Ruby glints of glazed cranberry,
Caught in sugar braids finely spun
For resurrection's anniversary.

But who's that lurking in the bush?
A winter-starved hungry beaver?
No! It's the mad Québécoise poised with cleaver!
She needs not the merest push
To leap out swiftly from her hide
And dispatch our bunny with visible pride.
She'll rush back home to her waiting kitchen,
Where we might find her eagerly pitchin'
Every vegetable known to man
Into her cast iron frying pan
To create the most sumptuous bed
To which our bunny shall be led.

So if you miss Bunny Rabbit this year,
Just come and dine on him right here.

Rubaiyat Revisited*

Your dog, your chair, your Mamirolle** and you
Are all I think of as I bumble through
These summer days before I *see* you too.

Your dog is better than a loaf of bread.
Her eyes will go silkily to my teeming head.
Crumbs would just clutter my clothing up instead.

Your chair is better than a jug of wine
Because, when in it, I shall sprawl-recline,
And no one will know a transport quite like mine.

Your Mamirolle can momentarily
Appease my need for verse; its colloquy
Strikes with a speech of tasteful subtlety.

So I'll pamper your puppy and wallow in your cheese
And, in your chair, adore you as you please.

---

* The *Rubaiyat*, a poem by the Persian mathematician Omar Khayyám (ca. 1050–ca. 1123), as translated by Edward FitzGerald (1809–1883), includes the lines: "A Book of Verses underneath the Bough,/A Jug of Wine, a Loaf of Bread—and Thou."
** A French cheese produced under license in Quebec.

Distraction

She:

I'm supposed to be
Cooking a rabbit,
But I've caught
An intrusive habit
Of jotting down
Lines for verse,
Or searching round
In my purse
To pay the opera season.
Dear man,
Can I have lost my reason?

A Widow's Pride and Joy

She:

An old widow's
Puny force
Cannot divorce
The handle
From the helix
Of her meat grinder.
She fears scandal
Will find her
Asking Felix*
To apply
His strength.
She tries to store
The coupled parts
In their drawer.
No luck.
Won't fit.
At length
She spies
The perfect perch,
Before her eyes,
Mounted
On the window frame:
Pencil sharpener,
Crank to the west.
Grinder's helix
Notches into
Sharpener's strut,

---

* The teenager who cuts the grass of the speaker of the poem.

Complicit fix—
Aesthetic balance
With grinder's handle
To the east!
She heaves
A sigh of thanks
At this felicitous pairing
Of helices
And cranks.

Last Night

Last night, upon the slightly spotted skin
Of the back of your firm and fully formed neck,
I placed a not quite unobtrusive kiss,
Designed to do no more than show affection.

But now in the morning's maelstrom, when you're in
Perpetual motion as you make a break-
Fast with nothing overcooked or hit-or-miss—
I'll show my gratitude for your selection.

Pests or Guests

She:

One day in the year two thousand and two
I vacuumed fifteen hundred ladybugs
And flushed them down the loo.
Asiatics, they were, brought in to help
With crop blight and such.
Not the two-dot darlings
We used to welcome
Marching the page fringes
Of what we were reading.
Haven't seen a two-dot in years.
I mourn their loss. My mind unhinges
When the multidot orientals
Drop into the salad I toss.
Hoping to pass for ornamentals
To my carefully selected greens?
Two-dots were never so unseemly.
They trotted their stuff serenely.

That day, when the score
Reached fifteen hundred Asiatics,
Possibly more, I snapped.
They rained down from both attics.
My vacuum cleaner wand
Inhaled the ceilings' seething harvest.
One, trapped between shirt and skin,
Bit me painfully on the breast.
War declared! I shall neither rest
Nor relinquish my domain,
Nor will I tolerate their fouling

Of my lunchtime salads,
Nor sing them my exquisite ballads.
I asked my neighbours what they do.
"We use poison; why don't you?"
Apparently, there's a spray
Which keeps the little beasts at bay.

But toxic warfare comes with risks
To cats and dog and to me.
(I surely have no wish to be
A lodger in oncology.)
I think myself kind and gentle,
Not Hitlerian, demental …

And the gracious hostess I shall play,
Welcoming guests night and day.
Winter barbecues on the stove,
Whirlpool baths with lotsa suds:
Pampering's quicker than natural death.
These pest controls should suffice
To keep the increase well in hand
And give me pause to catch my breath.
Our life together could be … nice!
Mr. M. might think me cruel,
But he's not tasted ladybug gruel.

April Harvest

She:

Today marks
The second time
I've photographed
A haul
Of ladybugs*
In the toilet
Before flushing
Them onward.
Why shoot
These unfortunates
Twice?

One day
Ten years ago,
Perhaps more,
I gathered
Nearly two thousand.
They floated above the white porcelain,
Awaiting their final journey …
To the sea.
A thought struck:
No one would believe this.
Click!

Today's digital shot
Went the rounds
Within the hour

---

*   All those ladybugs were harvested from the kitchen.

At show and tell
In my playgroup.
They all ask
The same question:
"Why not call in pest control?"
I doubt that poison
Is good for the
Soul.

Wooing

Perhaps I Should

She:

I wonder if,
In dreams, you've seen
Me come to you
In flowing folds
Of grape-de-sheen?
The cosmic hair°
For once in place?
The throngs of men°°
In deep disgrace?
If dreams were full
Of vitamin L,
Then should I dream
Such dreams as well?

°   Mentioned in "Refusing the Role," David Murray, *Summer in September and Other Poems*, Blooming, IN: iUniverse, 2016, p. 43.
°°   Mentioned in "Seeing and Hearing," ibid., p. 42.

Many Thanks

She:

I've told you often how
You bring out the best in me.
I'll tell you baldly now:
The worst, too, you can set free.

A murmured craving for G & S,*
And off you dash to HMV.**
Under your breath, "Yes, yes, yes!"
Coming up trumps, 1, 2, 3.

And how do I show my thanks
For doing my bidding near Dundas station,
For overworking your tired shanks
And loading you down with treasures' tribulation?

Do I send you vases of showy flowers?
Golden trinkets from Midas' cave?
Heavy volumes to weight your hours?
No! I treat you as my personal slave.

And shrivelling with a burning shame
From having brought you oh so low
(Exploitation was *not* my game),
I'm writing this to let you know

Your efforts find favour in my sight,
And also to wish you a restful night.

---

*   Gilbert and Sullivan, librettists and composers of operettas.
**   A major store selling recorded music.

Reply to "Many Thanks"

Your joy in reading subway maps
Is what inspires my sending you,
Along with clippings of articles,
A chart of new construction due.

I've sent you books and scads of words
And cuttings from the news,
As well as occasional DVDs
And compact discs you'd choose,

But now I'm sending a neighbourhood map
That includes an LRT*
And a plan for lots more buses on routes
Where more of them should be.

It's a future map for my neighbourhood
Where, I am daring to hope,
The rarefied joys that I have felt
With you might telescope

Into a screenplay of delight,
Where every day is new
Because you hold in your heart the key
To Sonnet Fifty-Two

By Shakespeare, where he says that feasts,
Being rare, are more enjoyed
Than routine meals on routine days
Of highlight points devoid.

---

* Light rapid transit: an above-ground suburban train that might replace a subway.

But such a wasteland could not be
On days when I'm with you,
When a smattering of your usual talk
Will fill me full right through

And a daily viewing of your eyes
Would lift each day to a year
Of gratitude endlessly refuelled
By seeing you standing near.

Heart and Mind

She:

Lub-dub, lub-dub, thy steadfast heart
Beats and pumps in constant flow
Thy blood, thy blood. Tho' we're apart,
Heart and mind, each evening's show
A three-ring circus doth present,
Hitching me to thy sentiment.

Nightmare and Prayer

She:

Could it possibly be
That I am gaining
A taste for heights?
The pedestal?
Does it suit me?
On phone call nights
The repeated raining
Down of praise …
Will it satisfy me
For the rest of my days?
Or will my appetite swell?
Expanding? Demanding
More sonnets? More odes?
Trowel-laden flattery?
Till, wits a-scattery,
I'll need a change of battery?

Please preserve us from such disruption
And deliver me from all corruption.

Your Portrait

When I in the morning's quiet your portrait see,
I ponder the strength and sleekness of your hair
And the firm lips that embed the harmony
Of your face as it upwardly faces me from where

Your portrait lies, deposited on piles
Of papers and of linens in a stack.
It's what I see first when morning files
Its entry when I pull the curtains back.

And I see it as my morning's masterpiece:
It is a photo'd picture from the press,
Reminding me of a black-and-white release
Of the contents of a retiree's address

Announcing that, although long years have gone,
Your image will stamp my years from my seventies on.

Compliant in Complicity

She:

"We can be
Compliant in complicity,"
You once wrote to me.
Then I thought,
Resilient in resiliency …
That, too, we can be.

Neither you nor I
Is yet resigned
To a future without
Our looking ahead
With gladdened eye
And clarity of mind.

Compliant in complicity:
A minuet or pavane?
Resilient in resiliency:
Jitterbug or cancan?
What the hell does it matter,
If we can keep up with the chatter?

We'll speak again soon …
Tomorrow at noon.

I Never Dreamed

I beat the woods and shrubberies of my mind
To flush ancestral thoughts from all their leaves,
Replacing ancient images of Eves
With avatars of modern womankind.

I never dared to dream, from childhood on,
That one like you would wend her way to me.
Your pleasant smiles and witty repartee
Unite with *caritas*, in grand communion

With sensitized alacrity and verve,
To answer the doting words I dare to fold
Into confessions of how I want to hold
You close as I can, while you, with steadfast nerve,

Allow me to adulate your mind as much
As your voice and eyes and devastating touch.

Appetite's Increase

She:

Yea, I shall slit
Thine envelopes
Wide, devouring
To the last bit
What lies inside.

What I Most Desire

How can I burn soft candles in a room
If you're too hard to see across the gloom?
Do I really want to see your eyes endimmed
By a flicker when a candlewick's been trimmed?
Can I really like the way your hair turns dark
When all there is to see by is a spark?

How can I see you whom I idolize
If candles burn so low, I strain my eyes?
How can I write my praises of your mind
If the room's so dark, I'm very nearly blind?
And how can I catch in cinematic glow
Your movements if the candlelight's too low?

Such fadings must be fought with ambient fire;
To see you radiant is what I most desire.

Taunt

She:

Tonight ... yes, tonight!
Those periwinkle crabs*
Will swirl sideways
About my knobby knees,
Taunting you with distant ease.
They'll never know
The hand that grabs
As round and round they go.
Their grey knit playground
Will hang loose from my bones.
Wary of you, not forgot,
They will circle the hem,
Seeking sheltering stones,
Where you will not
Ever catch them!

---

* The poems speaker refers to her light grey nightgown, featuring above the
  hemline a border of pale violet crabs.

Separate and Together

She:

The space between us
Shrinks and expands
With each tick
And each tock
Of my Seth Thomas
Kitchen clock.

You by your lake
And I by my stream—
Both of us know
These waters will mingle
In the salt sea,
No longer single.

Let Me Immerse You in Receptacles

Let me immerse you in receptacles
Of amorous verse that makes you want to blush.
Your absence only makes my yearning stronger,
And so I run the risk I'll get the push.

But were it not this way, and emptiness
And effort were to scorch my surging lines,
Nothing would survive of them save cinders,
Ashes of unfinished Valentines.

Not Dallas Bound

She:

Who'd ever
Want to go
To Dallas,
Where they
Have no
Aurora borealis
And possibly
Too much phallus?

Reply to "Not Dallas Bound"

I'd never want to go to Dallas
Unless I lived in a sultan's palace
Where you were a gorgeous grown-up Alice
And I was the Cheshire cat.

You, Dancing

To say I see
Your merciless beauty in the dark
Is a paradox that has no spark.

To say I hear
The silent marvels of your voice
Is rot in which I can't rejoice.

To say I feel
Your touch when you're away from me
Is quite devoid of gallantry.

But yes, I savour
Enchantment when your arms are bared
In eloquent dancing unimpaired

And clarity and clearness ricochet
From every body part you care to sway.

Valentine 2017

She:

May I never be weaned from your wooing!
The void would be too great
To leap in a single bound.
I've no desire to be shampooing
Your swirling seductions of late
From my tresses all adowned.
Keep on talking down the telephone line,
And keep me, please, as your Valentine.

My 2017 Valentine

Grey and silver coat the standstill lake
On this, a day so far from being warm
That even a pallid sunshine cannot make
Me venture into this aftermath of storm.

Instead I stay inside and idly think
How pleased I'll be to watch your active form
Potter between my countertop and sink,
Ensuring your cuisine will outperform

Criteria first encountered on your way
To making masterpieces that conformed
To culinary norms of yesterday.
But, over time, your skills have been transformed.

This Valentine upgrades all older praises.
Your artistry now relentlessly amazes.

Reply to "My 2017 Valentine"

She:

Heaven's sake!
Blingy hearts* for the gal,
Thanks to her pal
On the lake.
She basks in praise,
Is transformed in warm storm
Performed true to form.
Her heart swarms in blingy haze.

---

*   The Valentine card I sent her glittered with magnificent crystal hearts.

Health
and Age

Though Age May Dim ...

Though age may dim your summer-freshened youth,
It adds maturity, just as the spreading veins
Of a leaf lend added structural strength.

And though your sleep be shorter now than then,
An early morning's drizzling light becomes
A herald that shines before the showers begin.

And though you may strain a little more to don
Slippers or socks or whatever sandal leather
Covers your splendid feet, you still move on.

And though impatience strikes like a tiny chime
Of protest as the morning hours go by,
You keep your cheeriness despite the time.

And these are the reasons why I always want to stay
As close to you as firmly as I can,
Because you help me push old age away.

A Moment

I recently thought of the moment when you sat
Upon my sofa in my living room
And told my apartment supervisor that
He should take care when he began to groom

With herbicides my balcony's overgrown
Mantle of weeds that made, within the earth
Enshrined in the crevices between each stone,
Strong stems to guide their spread and height and girth.

He should take care, you said, to keep me free
From vapours that could cloud my vocal tract.
A ripple of admiration ran through me,
So timely was your show of nerve and tact.

Food for Thought

She:

Your recent mishap with the teeth
Left me more aware
Of what my teeth do every day
Free from any care.

Tonight I ate a mushy meal,
But it still required teeth.
Unchewed havoc in my gut?
Such pain defies belief!

Robert* had no teeth at all,
And yet he relished steaks!
I asked him how he managed:
"Good gums is what it takes."

All these years I thought 'twas gums
That adapted with their calluses,
But now I think perhaps 'tis guts
That deserve our lifted chalices.

_____

*   A mutual friend from the past.

With You

With you I want internally to exist,
And when our ageing physiologies
Subside in the slow downhill to slipp'ry death,
Long may that want sustain my aim to please.

The Way I Feel at 72

She:

Sometimes I feel like the devil,
So what does that make of me?
I suppose, on the basest level,
I'm between myself and the deep blue sea.

But on other levels I feel all lovely
Soon after talking with thee,
As a star in the calm night ocean
Reflecting what's far above me.

More often I feel like neither.
I simply feel like me:
Neither brilliant nor wicked, but wiser
Than I ever used to be.

The Way I Feel at 79

Sometimes I feel like an idiot saint
Who thinks he's better than he is,
When all that really moulds his acts
Is fear of penalties.

And sometimes I feel I'm the luckiest guy
In the world because we've met;
You bring a gusto to my life
Unknown to me as yet.

But often I feel like neither.
I'm simply poet me:
Not saintly or lucky,
Just happy to feel free.

A First Night of Deep Sleep ...

Immortal are all questions in romance:
No matter what one's age or century,
A slight disquiet or a dissonance
Within *oneself* evokes an enquiry
From whence it came, when it'll go, and whether
It's just about oneself or the two together.

My thoughtfulness comes from a circumstance
So rare, I'm forced to tell of it right here:
I awoke this morning in a sort of trance
At seven, unwilling and loath to rise and steer
Myself to my kitchen and coffee machine and snack—
So great was my unwillingness, I snuzzled back

Into the covers and slept till half past nine,
When one small question fuddled up my brain:
Was this because last night, in mood benign,
I'd basked in listening to the low refrain
Of your unrivalled voice as gently you suggested
That in the evening *no* coffee be ingested

In order to ensure my night-long sleep?
Yes, I had heard you. And now, while slowly awaking,
I feel how your suggestion has landed deep
Within the byways that my thoughts were taking.
So, was my sleep entirely biochemical?
Or one more proof of your charms alchemical?

The Next Night

Why do these lines give sleep such prominence?
Last night, I felt a burst of tiny growth
Of new desire to sleep and quickly fell
Into an instant Well of Death of Nothing
Till thirst sent me awake at 5 a.m.
I slowly drank a purchased juice made up
Of guava, of kiwi and of mangosteen.
Then back to bed I went till, tired,
I woke up after nine, like yesterday.

But I want those *words* to show more interplay.
No placid sleep could ever have inspired
Such arduous thoughts and contours as Byzantine
As my desire to *fête* and polish up
Each word until it flashes like a gem.
I want each word to carry greater meaning
And any fears to secretly dispel.
And rhyme I crave because it gives us both
A foil to counter prose's dominance.

Any Old Broom Will Do

She:

No cellophane on the line tonight.
Can it be I heard you right?
You yearn to stay young?
Miss the merry farce of ageing?
Never from our vantage gauging
The yingy-yangy, clinky-clanky
Clumsy stumble, rough-and-crumble—
Not too rough, lest we tumble
Headlong from old age into loathsome dotage,
So suited to our years?
(I scarce believed my ears!)
No shame attaining decades by the score!
Let's wear them with grace and slow the pace.
Such fun to sweep the floor
Free of youth's inanities
And strew upon it our own insanities!

Clutch of Time

I feel time clutch at me to make my rising
Clumsier than was my privilege
Years ago, when sunny mornings threw
Tumbles of light upon my windowpane.

Sunny mornings are still worth rising for,
No matter how often clumsiness reveals
How time can put its ham hands onto muscles
And twist an early rising into pain.

Keeping Ahead of Staying Afoot

She:

Winter's metronome I cannot abide!
Ice hidden beneath the latest snow
Minces my usual easy stride
Into the fussy sixteenth notes
The season's metronome decrees.
I scarcely dare to stray my eyes
To where juncos, redpolls and chickadees
Peck at grain that, broadcast, lies
But metres from my mincing feet.
Well Vivaldi knew the scurrying pace
Required to keep us upright, decorous and neat.
A fall at our age entails more than mere disgrace.
So unsightly, the snow, stained red as geranium
With contents of a blood-laden cranium.

Reply to "Keeping Ahead of Staying Afoot"

It's wintertime; I'm scared that you might fall.
So many possibilities multiply
Into catastrophes; I dare not try
To triage and classify them all.

What I do know is that here, in my head,
A bludgeon hovers over all Quebec
Whenever I think you're prone upon your deck
Or wounded on icy steps, staining them red.

And I, so far away, won't know your plight
Unless I hear, days later, you're not there
Where once I breathed with you the splendid air
Of an August filled with cavalcades of light

That made Arcadia of every day
While cedar waxwings tweeted getaway.

No Virus at the Opera

She:

Didn't wake up late.
Rose well before eight,
Rotten nose a-streaming.

Nabucco yesterday—
Too recent anyway
To catch but tuneful dreaming.

To catch a winter cold,
I must take hold
Of viruses a-teeming,

Giving them some days
To germinate and raise
Progeny a-scheming

To invade my DNA,
Reduce me to dismay
And whimpery blaspheming.

Didn't take a chance
On symptoms' advance.
Downed grapefruits redeeming.

Turns out you're right:
Cold and dry last night.
Better it were steaming.

How do I know
That this is so?
No sore throat a-screaming

With searing pain.
So once again
My health badge is a-gleaming.

Birthday Poem to You, 2016: You Have Not Been Accosted

I'm tempted, yes, to sympathize
With women of a certain age
For whom new birthdays symbolize
New evidence that the years will wage
Increasing war on legs and hair and eyes.

But when stark Age accosted you,
It only made your legs look longer,
It only made your eyes more blue,
It only made your hair the stronger
The greyer and more silvery it grew.

But Age has given *me* a gift,
Presumptions that command my mind
To alchemize your words to swift
Flotillas of seagirt verse designed
To swell the oceans so they heave and lift.

Birthday Verse, 2017: Mancunian Man

She:

Mancunian man
Of fourscore years,
In June you can
Receive our cheers.

A jolly good show's
Accumulation
Deserves our heartfelt
Celebration!

Birthday Greeting, 2017: Never Trust an Atom

She:

I once heard it said,
"Never trust an atom.
They make up everything."
But trust, friend, instead
Those grey cells, stratum
Upon stratum, lingering
Layered in your brain.
"Memory" they call it.
Let no one disdain.
"Use it or lose it"
Is what they all say.
Choose it *and* use it
On your own birthday!

States of Mind

If Ever ...

If ever a poem I should write
That pleased you not, I'd be contrite.
I'd take my pen and write a scribble
At which I'd hope you'd take a nibble
And go away quite satisfied
That nothing was said that was offside.

Impatience No. 1

I seethe with impatience when my will,
Coursing along its preplanned path of light,
Is stopped by shadowed hands of circumstance,
Delays that bewilder me by not being expected
And countermovements threatening to spoil
All that my best-intentioned hopes had held.

There's nobody to blame or to accuse.
There's not a thing or god in visible sight
On whom to pour my execrations loudly.
I could as well ascribe a soul to a tree
As find a scapegoat for my irritation.
It's nothing but simple facts that arbitrate,

Albeit without a pinch of consciousness,
Between my personal wants and those of yours.
Events, not feelings, disperse my dreamed-of clouds,
Attenuating hopes of future happiness.
But when such doubts intrude on my composure,
Your voice's magic quells all my inquietude.

My Dust, Your Dust

She:

My dust seems to dodge and cavort
As tho' engaged in disorganized sport,
Whilst yours, I imagine, dormant lies
Supine and level then ossifies—
More like silt and less like fluff ...
Yours, composed of stately stuff.

Some Tiny Movements of Your Hands

Some tiny movements of your hands
Might signal they were reprimands,
But I would fill my biased head
With quite deluded countermands
That you came on to me instead.

Serious

All introspective wheedling I'll forsake
If it should clutter up the things we do.
I will not let old foibles try to break
The simple joie de vivre I have with you.
And I will replace, with strong and joyful song,
Baggage from my past that doesn't belong.

So let the whippoorwills enchant the night
With songs that soar to the moon's magnetic lure.
Let rampant gladioli sway in the light
Of breezy summers, enhancing your allure.
And let the eternal wheelings of the lark
Stand contrasted with the stillness of the dark,

And let whatever gnaws at me, unkind,
Be torn away from its foothold in my mind.

Impatience No. 2

You are a perfect anchorage for Beauty.
Beauty can sit by you and adore your head
And then, in *no* dereliction of her duty,
Peruse your breasts as if a newlywed.

And I, poor outward viewer, watch and wait
While Beauty venerates your sleeping eyes.
I stand forever patient, as if a gate
Might open at the faintest of your sighs.

Then Beauty stands upright and knowingly smiles:
She slowly walks to where I wait. I tense
And wonder what she'll do with all her wiles
To stammering me, quite shorn of common sense.

But then she vanishes. You sleep on while I
Watch, sentry-like, till dawn refills the sky.

Letter to the Bard

She:

Dear Mr. Shakespeare,
How dare you preach to me
Of wasted beauty,
Its loss to fear,
Of the April of my prime
And of beauty's legacy?

Bossy old bard,
A pox upon your sneer!
Life's no mere show,
Nor is barrenness a crime.
And so, Mr. Shakespeare,
Writes a baroness of rhyme.

Foot Fetishes

Foot fetishes propel, in magnitude,
A disproportionate number of pages in
Medical textbooks and pornographies
Purporting to map propensities to sin.

But you display, from tip of toe to heel,
Such magnitudes of proportional perfection
That thoughts of medical words and of perversions
Vanish, behind my walls of introspection,

To places outside my present state of mind:
You're here, and here you dominate my sight.
And every touch I fantasize or feel
Remagnetizes all my dreams of night

When, by your side, I fetishize your toes
As signposts to places where wonder overflows.

Whine

She:

There you are there,
Safe in your lair
From my attitude drear,
And here I am here.

Perhaps *not* an attitude,
Maybe mere lassitude,
But without much assistance
I do feel the distance:

There you are there
And … here I am here.

PS: Mumble, bitch, gripe.
           What godawful tripe!
           You've the right to decline
           To countenance whine.

Impatience No. 3

Yesterday, impatience played a part
In suppressing the better feelings in my heart.
Not caring that impatience had prevailed,
I'd blurted mine out then realized I'd failed
To understand how my ineptitude
Might serve to change the tenor of your mood.

I'll have to remember to stay calm and dumb
Whenever delays and irritations come
And neither of us is at fault. I'll keep
Thoughts of impatience buried really deep
Below the earthen layers of my speech.
I cannot bear to think those thoughts might breach

The sanctity we have of moral trust.
Such thoughts I must contain because I must.

Transition

She:

April's vapour hovers
Over white fields' expanse,
Melancholic mist
Partially masking
Last summer's dead,
Where butterflies
Again might chance,
Before our eyes,
The mating dance
For lovers.
Sluicing raindrops
Fall from eaves
Without asking
Who believes
In coming crops.

Lift!
Lift that drooping head.
Trust!
Trust your anchoring roots.
Thrust!
Thrust up your newborn shoots.
Grow!
Grow from down below
Through shifting pebbles
Of weeping ice,
Past months of melting snow.

Greet!
Greet the songbirds' trebles.
Live!
Live transition instead.

My Solitary Goldenrod

My solitary goldenrod has grown
And now, in September, has wonderfully bloomed
As if the whole of summer had entombed
Its memories of last winter, spent alone.

Its gold reminds me of the sunny hours
I spent with you in August, when we talked,
Your puppy ran, and lazily we walked
Surrounded by your wilderness of flowers.

Evening the Score

She:

I remember running down the stairs,
Catching the newel post,
Momentum swinging me left,
Reversing my southward descent,
Propelling me northward
Out the front door.

That was decades ago. Heaps of cares
Swept up and turned to compost.
But these days, I'm all but bereft
Of alacrity, no longer hell-bent
On rushing forward
In search of more

Adventure, more trysts, taking on dares …
No, today, tendons and muscles stiff as toast
Limit the burdens I can heft.
Compensation, perhaps heaven-sent,
Draws inner me outward,
Evening the score.

I still hurtle down those stairs
In my mind. Still swivel around that post,
Whizzing now, horizontally. More deft!
This old-age fantasy has lent me
Gleeful wings: I fly skyward
Where I can soar.

Impatience No. 4

I feel a furtive longing to imbibe
A potion that would fuel a diatribe
On how I beg impatience, on my knees,
Not to contaminate my restless pleas

With daubs uncommon to many a rarish word
That steer my solemn sentences toward
Expressions that might serve to jeopardize
What virtues I may have garnered in your eyes

Because of the sincerity of my verse.
Impatience would only render matters worse
Should accidents of happenstance delay
The onset of a hoped-for glorious day

When I can awake and look across at you
And know that you'll be there tomorrow too.

Disorder

She:

Cobbling my thoughts together,
I'd be lucky to sort them out
Within a week of winter Wednesdays.
On second thought perhaps,
Given a more realistic view,
Barring unforeseen mishaps,
'Tmight take a century in Timbuktu …
It could depend upon whether
I'm still in touch with you.

Fantasy

At night I often lie awake,
Thinking till morning's golden light,
Despite the fact you're by my side,
Asleep in the beating heart of night.

I often fear you'll try to go,
And wonder if you'd feel more free.
But I find such thoughts are overcome
Whenever you are near to me.

My darkling thoughts all disappear
When, in the morning sunlight's rays,
Your presence calms anxieties
And prompts pellucid flows of praise.

A Vision
in Black

Theme

The setting: a clump of sofas
Laid out in a tapas bar.

The occasion: a finding of food
After having walked too far.

The moment: you had to stand,
In pain from sitting too long.

The dream: to capture this vision
Of you in a stalwart song.

The detail: dark-dressed, you stood
Like an epic angel in black.

The effect: your necklace sparkled
If you moved to the side or back.

The goal: eight variations
On this spectrum of sensations.

Variation No. 1

You bring
A warming hand
To my iniquity.
I sin
In thinking of you so much
That your blurry hand wave
Seen through a dusky train window
Is taken by me
To be a beckoning
Toward an increasing propinquity.

I tried
To be only concerned for your comfort
When you had to stand up in that bar,
But your hands were so clearly perceptible
Touching your black tunic's sides
That I was besieged by a lechery
So crudely inappropriate,
Given your disability,
That I felt that I *should* be accused
Of transgression of dignity.

Variation No. 2

It's easy to imagine
You as peremptory exhorter
Standing alert and upright, commanding
A heroine's declamatory power
To sway the spirits of a wavering crowd.

But I suspect that you
Will find your eloquence stammers
Because you'll hear your audience's murmur
Of unembellished and unfeigned surprise
At how your presence, clad in velvety black,

Intrigues them all so much that your words become
Lost sonnets trickling silently to nothing
While the chorus of your audience sings out loud
Brava! on viewing the beauty embodied in you.

Vacillation

She:

Shall I shed a few tears
For my poor puny words
Trickling away
Through a wavering crowd
Which likes feasting its eyes
More than lending its ears?

Variation No. 3

Although I try to fight embedded age,
Little I do myself can crack its clutch.
But when I saw you in that cafe's light,
Dressed in a black I deeply yearned to touch,
Age fell away without any help from me.

But you were enduring, silently, physical pain
With a back so aching you didn't want to sit,
So you stood alert in a guise of healthiness
So genuine in look that I was fooled by it
And failed to spot my misinterpretation.

Your tunic fell to form a gentle flare
Below your waist; it subtly emphasized
How the architecture of your upright pose
Successfully concealed your compromised
Tranquillity, transforming you into a heroine

Illuminated by the cafe's light,
Arrayed against a confluence of sofas,
You, epitome of my ardent vision.

Variation No. 4

I'm looking at you with bemused perception.
Your strong artistic hands and fingers
Slice up the fruit so its aroma lingers,

And I see a symphony of black
Defining, in textile, your upper body's build,
And I'm staggered by the joy with which I'm filled.

Variation No. 5

A thing of bling is the Christmas star
I bought at Hudson's Bay.
Appended atop my Christmas tree,
It lends a steadying symmetry
To the lights and ornaments hanging free,
Or taut, or swinging, or slack.

Your necklace glowed as you stood in that bar
At the end of that wonderful day,
To present, to a thunderstruck, awe-filled me,
A grippingly colourful unity
Composed of your necklace's harmony
Of gold with your tunic of black.

Both you and my tree are concordant. Each forms,
In a world that grows cooler, a regime that warms.

Variation No. 6

Gone is an overbearing thunderscape:
Peace cascades between ascending clouds
To fill the full horizon with a flood
Of placid reds and golds and umber browns.
The sun descends, and Night unfolds its wings.

From where we sat in that dim café,
Slowly you rose until you stood,
Full-chiselled to a solid obelisk,
An elegant monument of sculptured black,
Golden necklace round your tunic's cowl.

I was turned tipsy and felt my feelings smoulder:
My every thrust of thought was to regale you,
To serenade your beauty with new nocturnes
Filigreed with bright memorial fragments
Of times when, proudly, I've admired you freely.

Lusty Landlord

She:

Who'd expect the lusty lad lurking
Beneath your suit and tie and poise?
A woman in black stands up—not smirking—
And inspires a flurry of poetic noise.

She rents your pedestal, enjoys your praise,
Bathes in iambics without cease.
She's learned to like your wooing ways
And prays, dear sir, you renew her lease.

Variation No. 7

The maples sugar life with springtime's sound
At March's start, when branches drip their weight
Of melting snow onto the sleeping ground,
And you awaken and stretch and walk and grow
Exultant as the days regenerate.

Back in that bar, you never had intended
To flush an impassioned epic from my brain.
You stood, wanting discomfort to be ended,
And stayed there in a posture meant to slow
The spread of any extra amount of pain.

But I saw your tunic's blackness re-impel
Your necklace to gleam exotic with its gold,
And there I saw a luminous parallel
To the blackened trunks that rain-swept maples show
When the rain has stopped and timorous clouds unfold.

And thus *you* augured, by being a vision in black,
How rain-dark winters will melt the white
Of snowy woodlands, while the nights pull back
Their shades to let the April's sunrise glow
Awaken your world to springtime and delight.

Variation No. 8

A hollowed-out book with a key in it
We saw in its museum case.
No doubt its purpose was quite legit,
But my devious thoughts saw fit to chase
Momentous finales in my mind
That made of the key something far less refined.

Was it a key to a treasure hold
That held spare coin to be secretly spent
On ambient ventures erotic and bold?
Or was it a key to a passage that went,
Clandestinely dark, from a room in a palace
To a place of escape that afforded less malice?

Or was it a key to the book itself?
Was it a symbol of writerly power
To take a reader out of herself
Into a world where nothing goes sour
And is eternity fused with pleasure,
And *volupté*, and *luxe*, and unlimited leisure?

That odd little key in that sacrificed book
Has stayed in my mind from our tour made months back,
And I now add my image of how you look,
Dressed in your tunic of sveltest black,
With your golden necklace, perhaps a key
To the fun and the frolic you awaken in me.

Hollow Book, Golden Key

She:

To have sacrificed a book
To a golden key
Seems to me
A deed that took
Anguished deliberation.

CPSIA information can be obtained
at www.ICGtesting.com
Printed in the USA
BVHW031215291019
562358BV00001B/38/P

9 781532 080487